DATE DUE			
OCT 20 '93			
OCT 29 '93			
NOV 5 '93			
NOV 24 '93			
DEC 21 '93			
JAN 28 '94			
JUL 25 '95			
MAR 25 '96			
31 '04			

16276

The FINAL FOUR

Published by Creative Education, Inc.
123 South Broad Street, Mankato, MN 56001

Designed by Rita Marshall with the help of Thomas Lawton
Cover illustration by Rob Day, Lance Hidy Associates

Photography by Allsport, FPG International, Photri,
Spectra-Action, Sportschrome and UPI/Bettman Newsphotos

Printed in the United States

Library of Congress Cataloging-in-Publication Data

McGuire, William
    The Final Four/by William McGuire.
        p.   cm.—(Great moments in sports)
    Summary: Discusses the championship round of the NCAA
basketball championships, including powerhouse teams, exciting
games, and outstanding players from past years.
    ISBN 0-88682-310-2
    1. National Collegiate Athletic Association Basketball Tournament
—History—Juvenile literature. [1. National Collegiate Athletic
Association Basketball Tournament—History.   2. Basketball—
Tournaments—History.]   I. Title.   II. Series.
GV885.49.N37G66   1989
796.323'6—dc20   89-27648
                                                        CIP
                                                        AC

The FINAL FOUR

WILLIAM McGUIRE

CREATIVE EDUCATION INC.

During the past ten years, the Final Four has become one of the nation's most exciting sporting events. Each year the three games played to determine college basketball's national champion has been a roller-coaster ride of fun and thrills. Buzzer-beating shots, heartbreaking turnovers, and dramatic rebounds have all contributed to a decade of lasting memories.

For those who dared to travel the nail-biting road to the 1989 Final Four, their experience was no different. The teams, the fans, and the cheerleaders all contributed to another carnival-like atmosphere. Even the host community of Seattle joined the fun. Known as the Emerald City, Seattle painted a yellow brick road to the Kingdome for the fans to follow. And on a dark and dreary night in April, this golden path led 39,178 fans to an event they would not forget.

It was the National Collegiate Athletic Association finals. The contest featured the University of Michigan Wolverines

Rumeal Robinson drives to the hoop.

against the Seton Hall Pirates. From the opening tip-off, the game was a classic and those in attendance appreciated every minute.

The Michigan faithful roared as Glen Rice launched the Wolverines to an early lead. The Seton Hall crowd responded wildly as the Pirates rallied from behind to send the game into overtime. Now, with only three seconds remaining in the extra period both sides moved to the edge of their seats for the dramatic conclusion.

With his team trailing by one point and having just been fouled Michigan's Rumeal Robinson stepped to the free throw line. Two made free throws would give Michigan the title, but if he missed the first, Seton Hall was the champ. This one great moment would decide the winner of the 1989 Final Four.

Glen Rice goes up high for two points.

6

Over the years, the battle for the NCAA basketball championship has produced many memorable occasions. The 1989 contest between the University of Michigan and Seton Hall University is just one example in the long history of this tournament. There have been many other great games, many other outstanding players, and many other great moments:

1939. In the championship's inaugural year, the University of Oregon won the national title by defeating the Ohio State Buckeyes 46-33. After the game, Buckeye captain James Hull was heard to remark, "Oh well, we were not interested in playing in this tournament anyway. It was just so new . . . unheard of."

1946. Two firsts occurred during this championship: Four teams coverged at the finals site for the first time, and Oklahoma A & M edged North Carolina 43-40 to become the first two-time winner.

1956. Behind the great Bill Russell, the University of San Francisco won its second consecutive NCAA championship by crushing Iowa 83-71. In doing so, the Dons became the first undefeated champion, compiling a 29-0 mark.

Being a part of the Final Four is the ultimate challenge for college players.

1963. "Oh my did it feel good," commented Vic Rouse after scoring the winning basket in the University of Loyola's upset victory over defending champion Cincinnati.

1969. UCLA won its third consecutive championship. Lew Alcindor won his third consecutive outstanding player award.

1974. "Those are the ones that really kill . . . ," reflected Bill Walton, after UCLA's string of seven consecutive championships was broken by Louisville 80-77 in double overtime.

1979. Earvin "Magic" Johnson versus Larry Bird. Michigan State 75, Indiana State 64.

1982. A young freshman named Michael Jordan hits a jump shot from the corner with just sixteen seconds remaining lifting the University of North Carolina over Georgetown, 63-62.

1985. "We must play an almost perfect game," commented Villanova coach Rollie Massimino before watching his team shoot 78.6 percent from the field to stun the defending champion Georgetown Hoyas, 65-64.

These are just a few of the many great moments the NCAA championship has given basketball fans since its beginning in 1939. Today, over fifty years later, the excitement continues. The players, the coaches, the cheerleaders, and the spectators all play a large part of what has become known as March Madness—three straight weeks of college basketball. Sixty-four teams all fighting for the right to be called national champions.

The band helps set the tone for March Madness.

In arenas, over the radio, or on television, anywhere a game can be seen or heard, the madness can be found. By the third weekend, sixty games have been played and only four teams remain. It is March Madness' final act—the Final Four.

During this last seventy-two hours, all attention will be focused on one location. More than 100,000 people will attend. More than 20,000,000 will listen, and more than 100,000,000 will watch, as four college teams will play three games to decide who is "Number 1."

The Final Four hasn't always captured so much attention. In fact, during the tournament's early years, many critics claimed the real national champion was determined by the National Invitation Tournament. The NIT, its supporters argued, which was formed several years before the NCAA championship, attracted the nation's best teams. In 1945, this debate was settled once and for all.

The site was New York's Madison Square Garden. The event was the Red Cross benefit game featuring NCAA champ Oklahoma A & M versus NIT winner DePaul. But the main attraction was seven-foot Bob Kurland against six-foot, ten-inch George Mikan.

Oklahoma A & M's Bob Kurland, or "Foothills," as he was known to his teammates, was college basketball's first seven-foot All-America. Long and loose-limbed, the athlete looked like a grown man among boys. "A glandular freak," Kansas coach Phog Allen remarked. Yet no matter how funny or awkward he may have looked on the basketball court, there was no question about Kurland's ability to play the game.

The tall players often lead their teams, like Patrick Ewing led Georgetown during the mid-1980s.

In coach Hank Iba's defensive scheme, Foothills was a dominant force. "Bob was the first player to bat the ball away on its downward arc," commented former DePaul Blue Demon coach Ray Meyer. "He even caught some and threw them out over the defense."

If Bob Kurland was the ultimate defensive weapon, George Mikan was the unstoppable offensive force. Mikan not only led the nation in scoring in both 1945 and 1946, he was also considered one of the game's premier playmakers from the center position.

"Mikan was the best feeder out of the pivot basketball ever had," commented one-time St. John's University coach Joe Lapchick. For Mikan, it was a skill developed by necessity. "When my opponents ganged up on me, that meant some of my teammates were free. So I started concentrating on handing off or passing to players breaking around me."

The Kurland-Mikan matchup was billed as college basketball's greatest game. It was a promoter's dream, and was given all the hype of a heavyweight championship bout. "The benefit game," recalled Kurland, "was a game with a lot of hullabaloo, to the point where everybody didn't sleep well. It was for what they called 'mythical national championship.'"

George Mikan (99) of DePaul University.

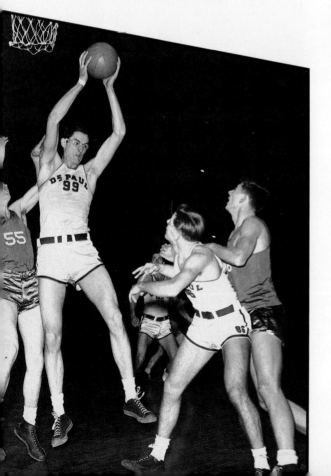

Despite the lack of sleep caused by excitement, players often rise above themselves in Final Four games.

Hullabaloo or not, reporters and fans came from around the country to witness this spectacular event. By the day of the game, over eighteen thousand tickets had been sold. New York's daily newspapers only intensified the interest. Who was better, they asked. The NCAA or the NIT? Oklahoma A & M or DePaul? Kurland or Mikan? That evening a standing-room only crowd packed the Garden to find out. Each had come to witness one of the greatest moments in NCAA history.

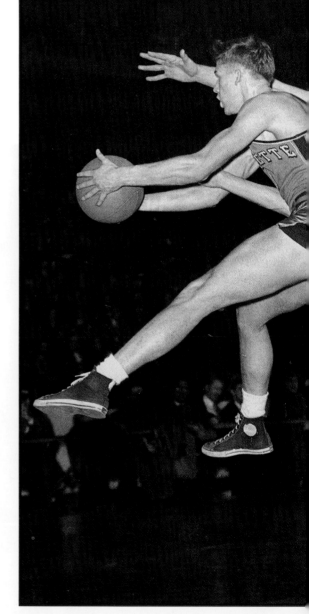

George Mikan (with glasses) shows his aggressive nature during a 1945 game with Marquette University.

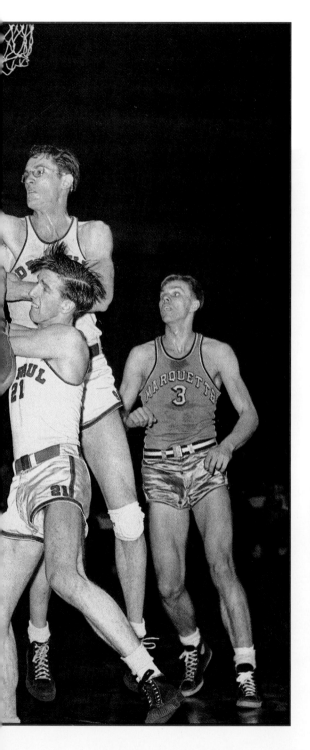

But what was promised to be "the game of the century" quickly turned into a disappointing display of basketball. The aggressive Mikan fouled out with only fourteen minutes gone in the contest, and "the rest of the game," remarked Kurland "was anticlimactic."

Indeed it was. Oklahoma A & M easily defeated DePaul 52-44, despite getting only fourteen points from Kurland. In the end, both Mikan and Kurland had been disappointing. Yet this forgettable game changed college basketball forever: The NCAA champion was now undisputed king, and the Kurland-Mikan duel had attracted a whole new audience to college basketball.

The Final Four champion becomes king of college basketball.

WILT THE STILT

Boosted by the hype surrounding Kurland versus Mikan, college basketball continued to gain popularity throughout the next decade. The Final Four, in particular, enjoyed growing support. But nothing equaled the attention thrown upon a young man named Wilton Chamberlain.

Without a doubt, the seventeen year old Chamberlain was the most publicized recruit in college history. As a towering seven-foot, one-inch high school senior in Overbrook, Pennsylvania, Wilt averaged over forty-five points per game, despite oftentimes playing only half the contest.

The amazing statistics drew virtually every college coach in the nation in pursuit of the giant teenager. At times it was overwhelming. "I'd come home from school," Chamberlain recalled, "and recruiters would be in my living room, there would be four or five letters on the bureau and my mother would tell me at least two people called long distance and would call back later."

The attention given Chamberlain didn't end with his decision to enroll at the University of Kansas; if anything it increased. His debut with the freshmen, in a meaningless preseason scrimmage against the varsity, attracted a crowd of more than fourteen thousand. And by the time Wilt became eligible to compete

Wilton Chamberlain chose to play for the University of Kansas, despite the efforts of many other colleges to recruit him.

with the Jayhawk varsity as a sopho-
more, the buildup was out of control.
"He'll be even more dominant than Bill
Russell," commented one observer. "He
shouldn't even bother to suit up," replied
another, "he should just report directly
to the Hall-of-Fame."

The predictions centered not only
around Wilt but around his Kansas team
as well. Most basketball authorities had
conceded the next three NCAA championships to the Jayhawks. It was an ex-
pectation that did not go unnoticed by
new Kansas coach Dick Harp. "Here it is
my first year as varsity coach and everybody believes that I will go three years
unbeaten. . . ."

It was this kind of pressure and these
types of predictions that followed Chamberlain and his teammates throughout
the 1956–57 season. The hysteria only
ended well after the last seconds ticked
off the 1957 NCAA championship, in
what is remembered as one of the greatest moments in the history of the Final
Four.

*"Wilt the Stilt" picks a rebound out of the air during a
1956 tournament game.*

The contest matched the University of
Kansas against the University of North
Carolina or, as the headlines declared,
"Wilt Chamberlain against the undefeated Tar Heels." Through regulation
time and two extra periods these two
squads battled to an even draw. It was
quite a surprise to most fans who had
anticipated a Kansas blowout.

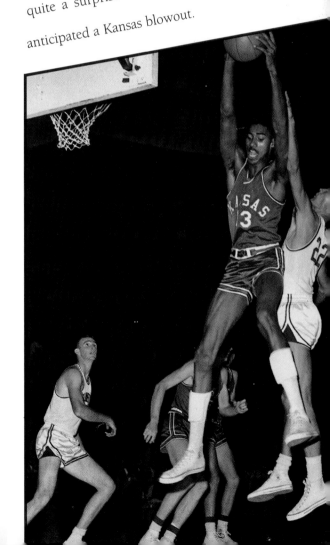

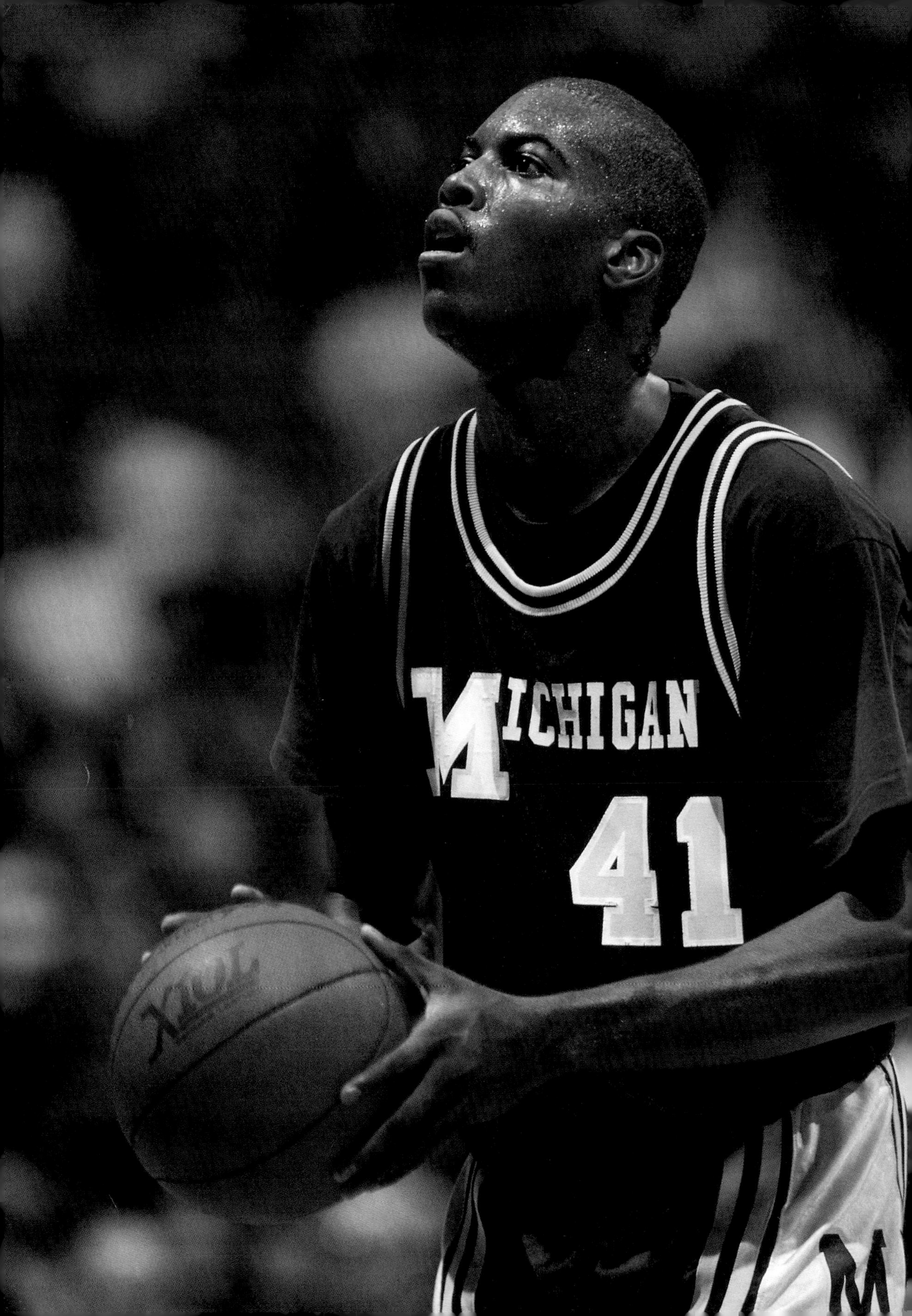
MICHIGAN
41

Now with only six seconds remaining in the third overtime, Kansas, as it had been all evening, was hanging on for dear life. Chamberlain's squad led 53-52, but the Tar Heel's center Joe Quigg had two free throws to steal the national championship for North Carolina.

Quickly, Quigg stepped to the line and sank his first free throw. The crowd barely had time to react. But now with the score tied, all the emotion and hysteria that surrounded Wilt and the Kansas Jayhawks was let loose. Wild cries and nervous cheers echoed through the arena. One more successful free throw and Goliath would be slain.

Calmly, Quigg stepped back from the line and wiped his hands. As the referee handed he ball to the Tar Heel center for his second attempt, the crowd held its breath. After several hard dribbles, Quigg lofted a high arching shot toward the basket. As the ball reached its highest point, every eye in the stadium looked toward the ceiling.

Glen Rice of Michigan gets set for a free throw.

Pages 20–21. North Carolina and Syracuse players position themselves for the rebound.

Then . . . just when it appeared as though the ball would remain suspended in midair forever, it swiftly rippled through the net and fell quickly to the floor. Wilt the Stilt had been toppled and the University of North Carolina Tar Heels were national champions.

THE WIZARD OF
WESTWOOD

The most difficult accomplishment in sports is doing what everyone expects you to do. Wilt Chamberlain and the 1957 University of Kansas basketball team are just one example of that: there are many others. Whether it be a team sport like basketball or an individual event like tennis, the pressure to live up to expectations is often overwhelming. That is why the record of John Wooden at the University of Los Angeles at California is so remarkable.

Between the years of 1964 and 1975, the UCLA Bruins and coach Wooden dominated the Final Four. In ten of those twelve years, the Bruins brought home the national championship. Year after year they were expected to win, and year after year they won.

The Bruins won in 1969 and 1972 with superstars like Jabbar and Walton. The Bruins won in 1964 and 1965 with versatile players like Goodrich and Erickson. And the Bruins won in 1971 with unheralded players like Steve Patterson. The one constant through it all was Wooden.

It made no difference who the players were, the "Wizard of Westwood" kept winning and winning and winning. His style dictated the results. It was a system based on upsetting and disrupting the opponent. Fast-break offense, ball-hawking defense, anything to antagonize the opposing team.

Page 23   Coach John Wooden and one of his most famous players after a 1968 tournament.

Yet it was a style of basketball that seemed to contradict the coach. Wooden was a gentleman on and off the court. He didn't smoke, drink, or swear at officials. In fact, Wooden seldom raised his voice.

One of his most famous players, Kareem Abdul-Jabbar, recalled that when Wooden got angry he would sternly say, "Gracious goodness. That's not how you do it."

Even his opponents, whom Wooden did so much to disrupt, admired his sportsmanship. "We were about to defeat the Bruins," commented Marvin Tommervik, the captain of the 1966 Washington State Cougars, "and after the game even before the clock had run out, he came over and congratulated our coach and each of those sitting on our bench. 'Nice game, good game,' he said. John Wooden could take it as well as dish it out."

Over the years, however, Wooden did a lot more dishing than taking. His teams became a national phenomenon. A Yankees', Celtics', Canadien-type dynasty that redefined the sport of college basketball. But considering all the victories, all the players and all the wonderful memories, the dynasty's last game may have been its greatest moment.

It was John Wooden's retirement game, the 1975 championship featuring UCLA versus the University of Kentucky. Just two nights earlier, after a dramatic overtime victory over Louisville, the sixty-four-year-old Wooden had told his club he was calling it quits. "I don't want to go," he remarked as his eyes met those of everyone in the room. "I have to. Doctors orders."

Though appearing fit, Wooden had not been sleeping well, and his personal physician had advised him to step aside.

His long reign at the helm of college basketball's best team would not end, however, before one last dramatic performance.

The first half of coach Wooden's last game was played at a hectic pace. There were fifteen lead changes and five ties. The second half looked like more of the same until the Bruins jumped to a twelve point lead at the midway point.

The NCAA Final Four is the showcase of college talent.   *The fast pace of college basketball makes it exciting.*

Courageously, the Wildcats fought back. With just over five minutes remaining in the contest, Kentucky had cut the UCLA lead to a point, 76-75. The Bruins seemed to have lost their poise, and the UCLA crowd had grown still. Had Wooden's club run out of gas?

John Wooden shouts directions to his players during his last game as a coach in the Final Four.

The next sequence of events as related by referee Hank Nichols would hold the answer:

"UCLA forward Dave Meyers took a jump shot and fell into a Kentucky guy, Kevin Grevey. I called the foul on Meyers, he slammed the ball on the floor, and I called a technical. That of itself was no big deal. The big deal was that John Wooden went absolutely nuts. My partner, Bob Wortman, had to hold Wooden back. I'd always heard what a gentleman Wooden was . . . I was surprised and shocked he was doing all this stuff at me. I didn't hear it, but I read it in the papers the day after the Kentucky game that Wooden came out there shouting, 'That guy's a crook and a cheat.' "

It certainly was an uncharacteristic move for the even-tempered coach. But in his last game, with the national championship at stake, the Wizard knew once again what it took to win.

From this past moment on, it was all UCLA. When the final buzzer sounded, the Bruins had defeated the Wildcats 92-85, and John Wooden had a retirement present like none other—his tenth national championship.

UCLA on the run.

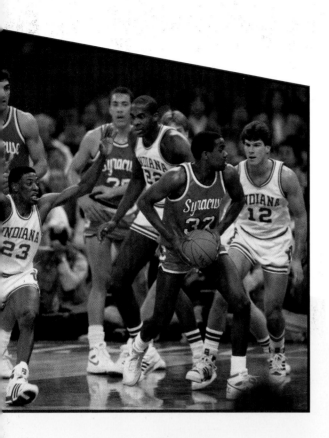

SUCCESS

Not one of the contestants—Indiana, Providence, Syracuse or Las Vegas—in the 1987 Final Four was playing for their tenth national championship in twelve years. In fact, only Indiana could claim to have captured even one NCAA basketball title. Nonetheless, the 1987 Final Four produced a championship game that would be long remembered.

Indiana Hoosiers vs. Syracuse Orangemen.

The contest featured the Indiana Hoosiers, who had defeated Las Vegas, against the Syracuse Orangemen, who advanced to the finals with a victory over Providence. More than fifty thousand fans packed the Louisiana Superdome to witness this exciting matchup, and no one left disappointed.

The game itself was brilliantly played, with both teams showing the talent and skills that had brought them to this night. Although the lead changed hands several times in the first half, Syracuse was seemingly in control. After hitting seven three-pointers in the first twenty-nine minutes, Indiana's leading scorer, Steve Alford, was shut down by the stingy Syracuse defense. Meanwhile, offensively, the Orangemen took control behind the explosiveness of Sherman Douglas and Derrick Coleman.

Midway through the second half, Syracuse, the pregame favorites, had opened an eight-point lead. The Hoosiers were in trouble, yet they would not quit. Behind the athleticism of junior guard Keith Smart, and several missed free throws by the Orangemen, Indiana battled back. With under twenty seconds remaining in the game, now trailing only by a point, 74-73, Indiana had the ball. Indiana had the opportunity to win. . . .

Steve Alford of Indiana puts up a jump shot.

Success isn't always being the winner; it isn't making a lot of money or covering your walls with trophies or getting your name in the newspapers and your picture on television, Bob Knight was saying. It's none of those things. "Success is performing to the limit of your potential," he said. "It's trying your level best so that you can look back and say to yourself, 'I did everything I possibly could.'

Fiery coach Bob Knight of Indiana.

"None of us ever quite get there. But we can try, by golly, we can try. And if a player I have coached can say to himself honestly that he gave the best that was in him, then he's learned something a lot more important than winning. He's learned how to win.

"There's a heck of a lot of difference. Winning is great. It's a wonderful feeling —the whole world is yours. But it only lasts a little while. What stays with you is knowing what it takes to play to the best of your potential."

. . . As the clock moved under fifteen seconds Indiana pushed the ball up-court. Patiently, the Hoosier players looked to Alford to get free. :12 . . . :11 . . . :10. But the Big Ten's second all-time leading scorer was not to be found. Quickly, the ball was thrown inside . . . :09 . . . :08 . . . :07 . . . and back out to Keith Smart with just six seconds remaining in the game. At that great moment, Smart let the Hoosiers last chance go. "I just tossed the ball up," said Smart. "I didn't know where the ball went."

Michigan players enjoy the winning feeling.

He soon found out. The ball went through the hoop and gave the national championship to the Indiana Hoosiers. After the game a surprisingly quiet Indiana head coach remarked, "We won't go down in history as one of the dominant NCAA champions . . . ," but this club did "play beyond its potential." From Bob Knight there could be no higher praise.

Like the 1987 Indiana Hoosiers, the 1989 Seton Hall Pirates had performed beyond anyone's expectations. They had been picked to finish no better than seventh place in their own conference and now, holding a 79-78 lead over the Michigan Wolverines, they were three seconds away from becoming national champions.

Standing in their way however, was a six-foot, one-inch junior guard from Michigan who had a one-and-one to give the championship to the Wolverines. But he had to make both.

Amid all the excitement and hysteria that is the Final Four, Rumeal Robinson quietly stepped to the line and did just that. Michigan was the new national champion. "I don't know whether to cry or not," Robinson reflected afterward. "It is a childhood dream to do something like this." In reality, it is one of the great moments in Final Four history.

Rumeal Robinson lays up two points during the tournament.